Investing

A Tested Roadmap To Discovering Who You Were Meant
To Be, Realizing The Dreams You Have For Your Life, And
Crafting The Kind Of Existence You Deserve

*(Investing In Growth Of Dividends And Management Of
Portfolios)*

Danny Wilder

TABLE OF CONTENT

Spend Your Money On Outside Developments.

Buying things that are unrelated to key turning points in history is yet another strategy for gaining respect. In a given scenario, an appraiser has the highest possible amount that he will actually want to evaluate the house for, and there is a very specific range of features for which people are willing to pay. For instance, if you buy a home in an area where there is a large variety of upsides of homes ranging from $200,000 to $600,000 depending on the parcel, house, and area, you may have the opportunity to find an undervalued home in this kind of region, and then you can increase the value of the home by making a few minor improvements. If you are a savvy shopper, you will want to take advantage of the many benefits that come with purchasing items that are not on the cutting edge of technological innovation.

Adding on an Extension to It

Home additions, which typically involve the demolition of an existing room such as the kitchen and the construction of a new room, an additional room, a sunroom or a later bathroom, are another way that the value of a house can be increased. This is especially clear in the event that you live in a high-cost zone, in the event that your home is maybe the smallest home on the square, or in the event that you dwell outside of an improvement in an area where property values vary a great deal. Your house will become more valuable if you install home improvements, but it will also become much more comfortable for you and your family, which is essential in many other ways besides just the financial ones.

Bear in mind that, unless you sell your property, this will result in an increase to your regularly scheduled installment. This should be your top priority. Examining homes that are comparable to the one you own or are considering purchasing is the most efficient method for determining whether or not an upgrade would raise the value of the property. You should request that your real estate agent or an appraiser provide you with continuing bargains that are comparable to those that are currently being offered in the area where you now live or are considering purchasing a house in. You should request that they provide you a sum that is equivalent to both the existing house and the expanded house as though the addition had been finished at that point.

Consider the following scenario: you are interested in buying a house in a location that is characterised by a high degree of topographical diversity that is 1,800 square feet and costs $220,000. Homes in the area sell for anywhere from $180,000 to $800,000 on average. The expert went over all the most recent bargains in the area with you and provided the following information:

Two weeks ago, a property with 1,500 square feet of space sold for $180,000.

Two months ago, a property that was 2,400 square feet in size sold for.

$460,000 A property with 2,800 square feet that was put up for sale a month earlier brought $540,000. A property with 3,200 square feet and six weeks ago sold for

$660,000

According to the model presented above, right from the beginning, it seems to be a higher quality private neighbourhood with rising home prices proportional to square footage.

When comparing two distinct homes, it is important to take into account a variety of factors, regardless of the location of the properties. These include elements like the area of the lot, the size of the parcel, the number of bedrooms and bathrooms, the layout, the kind of finishing touches like a pool or other amenities, and a variety of other factors. However, when you are comparing properties that are located in the same general neighbourhood, the location is the most important feature to take into consideration. It would be to your advantage to take a drive by several recently sold properties in the neighbourhood to get a sense of how the land and homes there compare to the one you plan to buy. This will ensure that everything works out for the best.

You can see that supposing you added on an additional 1,000 square feet, the house in the model above would likely be about $540,000, which is approximately $320,000 more than whatever you are hoping to spend for it. This is because adding on an additional 1,000 square feet increases the cost per square foot. Depending on where you live, this expansion will probably set you back about one hundred dollars per square foot, which comes out to a total cost of roughly one hundred thousand dollars. In the event that you were to carry out the enlargement and then sell the home, you would realise a profit of around $220,000 prior to any charges. Assuming you lived in the property for a significant amount of time and then sold it subsequently, you would not have to pay any expenses out of the profit you made from the sale of the property.

Statistics are a Myth:

Statistics are notorious for their ability to mislead. Information can be obtained that has no relation to the problem at hand, the origin of the data or the boundaries for the instances can be arbitrary, and errors in the information can lead you to believe something that is not true. There is no way for you to determine whether or not you are utilising the information correctly and coming to the correct conclusion.

In secondary school, I was not a fan of the vast majority of my classes; but, there was one year when I participated in an advanced placement (AP) insights course, and the knowledge I gained there has stayed with me ever since. Regardless of whether or not my instructor anticipated it, one of the things that I took away from the course was how ridiculous and off base so many different perspectives are. It's not usually the statistics itself or the information itself that matter; rather, it's the interpretations that different people come to regarding the numbers and the information. (This thought also assisted me in coming to the realisation that things in life aren't always what they appear to be, which turned out to be an important insight.)

One of the models from the class that I have generally been able to recall is a measurement that stated something to the effect that something like 95% of auto accidents occur within a radius of five miles from an individual's residence. The readership came away with the realisation, which is entirely appropriate given the circumstances, that they ought to have increased their level of vigilance when driving closer to their homes because it was significantly more likely that they would be involved in a collision at that point. The objective of the test that we were given in the class was to look for any hidden information concerning the measurement that might have caused the information or the translation to be wrong.

Are you able to spot the problem with the statistic?

The reality was that at that time and in the region where the measurement was taken, a significant number of people rarely travelled more than five miles away from their residence. This was true in both of those places. So the reason why the measurement indicated such a high risk of accidents within a five mile span was not because it was more hazardous to drive nearer to home, but rather because the majority of driving was done within a five mile span. This was the true explanation for why the measurement showed such a high likelihood of accidents within a five mile span. It is obvious that the majority of accidents take place there due to the fact that persons weren't driving anywhere else at the time.

Since then, nearly every statistic that has been presented to me has been met with my scepticism. I don't address this because I need it to be incorrect, but rather than just accepting the conclusion as fact, I make sure there isn't any hidden information in the data or in the environment that could make the results inaccurate or even harmful.

Measurements might be astonishingly misleading for those who are interested in investing in fresh land. For example, it makes my stomach flip every time I see a magazine or blog provide the most up to date breakdown of 'excellent urban regions' for giving. This is because these lists are often based on subjective judgements of what constitutes a "good urban area." The titles of some ongoing storylines I've seen are as follows:

The 10 Best Places to Put Your Money Right Now

The Locations That Will Provide the Highest Returns to Real Estate Investors in 2023

The U.S. cities with the highest potential for positive cash flow are listed below.

The top ten cities in the United States with the most rapid population growth

The one that drives me absolutely bonkers is any title that remotely resembles the second item on the previous list, which is titled "The Most Profitable Cities for Real Estate Investors in 2023." My body contorts into a gripping motion whenever I come across something like this in my reading. This is because to the fact that I am aware that a number of people will read it and, with the best of intentions, look to put their money into one of those urban communities. However, they will be completely unaware of how dangerously misleading the rundown of urban communities is likely to be.

The most serious issue with that kind of breakdown is that the author almost never specifies exactly what kind of contributing they are referring to when they make that kind of reference. The title of this article is "The Most Profitable Cities for Real Estate Investors in 2023," but what exactly does that mean? Is it accurate that they are considering the purchase of investment homes, or would they claim that they are considering the purchase of properties to flip instead? The fundamentals of contributing to investment property and flipping houses are very different from one another. Even while a city might be beneficial for either one or the other, this is not always the case. It's possible that a market that's great for investment properties won't be profitable for flippers, and it's also possible that markets that are great for flippers will be terrible for investors in investment homes.

Reading a rundown such as "The Most Profitable Cities for Real Estate Investors in 2023" makes me want to storm into the creator's office, point at the rundown, and then bash him over the head with it. I'm not a particularly aggressive person, but reading a rundown like this makes me feel like I should be more aggressive.

The reason I get so worked up about this is because new financial backers, and surprisingly some accomplished financial backers, don't have the foggiest notion what they don't have a clue about. This makes me very angry. They are completely oblivious to the possibility that these findings are grossly misleading. In addition, in a sector such as land contributing, incorrectly directing data can cost anyone a fortune.

Reading a summary of the information or a measurement is only meant to get you interested in doing further research. If you are interested in investing in rental properties for the purpose of generating cash flow, for example, and a city is mentioned as being one of the greatest places to invest, you should investigate whether or not that city actually generates cash flow. There's a good chance it doesn't work out that way. The author was probably considering which urban locations are the most secure and likely to appreciate, although stability and potential appreciation do not typically have an effect on cash flow.

Under no circumstances should you run with the facts or ideas that anyone else shares. If you are actually interested in the information, you should learn more about the context in which it is planned, compare this information to the fundamentals with which you are already knowledgeable regarding your particular project procedure, and determine whether or not the two pieces of information fit together correctly.

Making a Presentation to the Landlord

This is the most challenging aspect of rental arbitrage because, despite the fact that it is very simple to search for a house and determine whether or not it is suitable for Airbnb, there is still the matter of whether or not the landlord would agree with your idea.

Now that we have everything out of the way, let's discuss the most vital aspect of this book, which is How to Pitch a Landlord. For the purpose of this section, we will provide a brief overview of what it requires to pitch a landlord for Airbnb, as well as a few fast pointers on how to do it, in the hopes that you will be able to pitch a landlord and get that

YES. The following are the steps that will lead to a successful landlord pitch:

1. Have a solid understanding of the company. This is a very important component of pitching, as you want to give the impression to the landlord that you are an expert who is familiar with all aspects of the company. You wouldn't want to meet the landlord and give the impression that you don't know what you're doing, because the landlord will almost surely have a lot of questions, and if you want to be successful, you'll need to have answers to all of those questions. Therefore, it is necessary for you to be informed of the associated fees and expenses, as well as the regulations of the city and the insurance plans. Since

Airbnb offers a host protection coverage worth $1 million, you will want to make sure that you reassure the landlord that his property will be secured with host protection insurance worth $1 million from Airbnb. In the event that a property sustains damage, Airbnb will be responsible for paying the associated costs. You will also require a business plan to assist you in demonstrating to the landlord how you intend to conduct the business. When it comes time to answer the question of how you will really operate the firm, the plan will come in very handy. The landlord could inquire things such as, "How do you intend to go about doing that? They will ask you, "How are you going to bring all of these people?" and you will have to explain to them that you realise the advantages and disadvantages of having guests as opposed to tenants. Because you are essentially trying to sell the idea that Airbnb visitors are often better than tenants to the landlord, having a solid understanding of the company is extremely vital and fundamental. Be aware that when a landlord rents out their property and the tenant's lease is up, the landlord is responsible for going into the property and fixing all of the damages done by that tenant. On the other hand, guests staying at an Airbnb property basically just check in, lodge, sleep, cook, shower and so on, and then check out, leaving the property in excellent condition.

In order to effectively compare Airbnb visitors with tenants, you will need to have a lot of positives and drawbacks to compare, which means that before you pitch, you will need to do your research and thoroughly understand the business.

We've Got a Long Way to Go!

We are merely scraping the surface of what this expansive idea of the metaverse has to offer, as many analysts have pointed out, and promising prospects will continue to emerge in the future.

Online gaming has typically given us a taste of what this enormous sector has to offer in terms of cross-cultural networking, virtual platforms, and the building of community in a pervasive virtual world.

In spite of this, the value that might be derived from the Metaverse is virtually unbounded because to recent advances in technology.

Investors who are interested in truly unique cryptocurrency projects should go further than the idea of a virtual universe.

The Metaverse is a platform for connectivity "and has utility beyond sectors, from reforestation to energy and environmental projects, games, and engaging new forms of digital engagement, which enables individuals to utilise their acquired digital products in a manner that is both distinctive and functional.

Will We Actually Be Able to Use the Metaverse?

The world's largest information technology companies are making their grand entrance into the Metaverse. Microsoft has aspirations of creating a corporate metaverse, while Mark Zuckerberg, CEO of Facebook, is fully invested in the Meta project.

In the meantime, social gameplay has become a widespread phenomena because to the rise of multiplayer online videogames such as Fortnite, Minecraft, and Roblox. These games create technologies that have the potential to serve as the foundation for the creation of the Metaverse. Roblox, the boxed game that is popular with children aged seven to twelve, is considered by several game developers to have the potential to become the most effective metaverse environment in the years to come. On the other hand, Minecraft is run on Hadean cloud software, which has the capacity to support thousands of users on a single planet.

The Hadean software that powers Minecraft has the capacity to support thousands upon thousands of users.

The computational capacity necessary to deploy virtual reality technology to a massive scale is only just becoming available now. Companies that focus on decentralised computing, like Improbable and Hadean, have the ability to connect ten thousand gamers to the same server at the same time. Just a decade ago, the idea of hosting fifty thousand people at sporting events and concerts at the same time would have been unthinkable. However, several companies working in the metaverse are considering doing just that.

The process of buying and selling products in the Metaverse is made easier by the use of non-fungible tokens and cryptocurrencies, which opens the door to new commercial opportunities. But what is even more important is that, in the end, these tradable tokens will make it possible for you to move your digital identity and commodities between different metaverse realms. For instance, you will be able to change the pixelated sword you used in a certain Robloxvideogame into a lethal gun that you can use in Fortnite.

When this occurs, the Metaverse will have fully transitioned into the "meta" state, and you will be able to move between levels with the same ease as in works of science fiction such as "Ready Player One" and "Snow Crash." Consider the decade of the 1990s, when mobile devices for the first time made it possible for individuals to communicate one another across a variety of platforms. During this time, mobile communication went beyond anyone's greatest imaginations.

The Expansion Of Potential Avenues For Monetary Gain

The development of the devices that are used to consume music today, which go beyond the first tool, which is the smartphone, and the new social segments, such as the short-form video, suggest that the rise of revenue prospects is still in the early stages at this point.

Therefore, record labels have undergone a metamorphosis and have developed a whole series of specialised skills that associate the artistic aspect, namely the search for new talent, with the skills related to technological innovation as well as the capability to accompany and assist their artists in this complex evolutionary scenario. This has caused the labels to take on a new appearance.

This continual innovation is certainly not confined to the recording business, but it will also have an expanding impact on the world of music and writing, where technology will become increasingly common in the creative process and in the segment dealing with royalties administration.

Last but not least, the context of world evolutionary history should not be overlooked. When compared to the most innovative markets, many developing nations are still in the beginning stages of the consumption of streaming music. However, according to the forecasts, even in continents such as Africa and

Asia, the trend will follow that of the United States of America, Europe, and China. In this respect, the expansion of streaming platforms in India, such as Gaana, and Africa, as well as the emergence of new local artists of the new generations ever closer to innovation and ready to ascend the global rankings, are examples of the additional potential associated to local technical partners.

The transfer of value can be done quickly and with relatively little fees when using cryptocurrencies. Because of this, they are frequently used for transferring money across international borders.

- Cryptos are freed from the control of professionals and cannot be preserved in cold storage

- Some people consider them to be the money of the future. • Some supporters like how digital currency eliminates national banks from dealing with the cash supply because national banks have a tendency, over the long haul, to diminish the value of money through inflation. • Cryptocurrencies are worldwide, which means they have the same value in every country. • Cryptocurrencies are traded from one individual to another on the internet without a middleman.

- Bitcoin exchanges are completely untraceable and confidential.

- Fees so low as to be negligible

• Rapidity • Stability without Inflation •
Freedom from Payment Obligations • It
is beyond the power of the central
legislatures to take it away.

Cryptocurrencies have a number of
drawbacks, including the fact that the
future of digital currency is uncertain.
Investors that need to make predictions
in this market should most likely stick
with the most well-known brands, such
as Bitcoin, Ethereum, and Litecoin. • A
record equilibrium can be cleared out
because digital currencies are virtual
and lack a central storage facility. This
enables a record balance to be cleared
out. In the event that a customer
misplaces the private key to their wallet,
any digital currency that they possess
will no longer be retrievable.

• Con artists can also take over someone else's portable record by pretending to be the current holder of the record.

• A great number of people are still unfamiliar with cryptocurrencies • It's possible that the government may try to block progress. It is possible to prohibit them.

• Absence of legal redress • Participation in unlawful tax avoidance and the black market

In order to purchase cryptocurrencies or other types of digital money, you will need a wallet, which is an internet application that can store your money.

After registering on a trade and transferring the necessary funds, you will then be able to purchase cryptocurrencies using those funds.

Use just a wallet that was produced by a reputable company. Carry out some study. The cryptocurrency exchange platforms Coinbase and Binance are two of the most prominent in the world.

If you need to buy bitcoin and other cryptocurrencies and then sell them again, there will be a few fees associated with the transaction. These fees include fees associated with the exchange, the shop, the withdrawal, and the exchange itself.

Lessons in Education That Are Both Powerful and Profitable

(1) Exercise an unusually high level of caution while working with lawyers or

judges. They have a more comprehensive understanding of the body of laws than you do, which puts them in a position to create a variety of issues for you.

(2) When a participant in an agreement makes a request to amend a phrase that appears to be innocuous in the agreement, you should give some serious thought as to the reason why they are acting in this manner.

(3) If you are acquiring multiple properties in the same area, try to close on all of them around the same time. This will prevent the last property from pressuring you into making a decision. Or, alternatively, one might follow Walt Disney's lead and buy each property under a different buyer name so that no

one would suspect that a single organisation was purchasing all of the properties. This would achieve the same goal.

7. Payment in Full in Cash

A seller who was about to close on a house that was worth $2 million hoped to back out of the deal after learning that another buyer was willing to pay $23 million for it. He was under the impression that he had devised a cunning plan to thwart the conclusion. The cash was to be given to the retailer upon the completion of business, as stated in the agreement. Therefore, when the time came for the closing, he demanded that the title company pay him in actual currency. He stated that in the event that he did not receive cash, he would not sign the paperwork. He would not acknowledge a wire move, a clerk's cheque or any other form of payment.

Ben, the buyer, and the title company were both very angry about the situation. Ben had to quickly come up with a response because there was only one day left until the date that the agreement was to be dissolved. If he did not, he would end up losing this mind-boggling arrangement. He dialled the number of his investor and inquired about the speed with which he could obtain $2 million in cold, hard cash. Ben instantly brought the investor up to speed on what the dealer was doing, which caused Ben's broker to be perplexed over the reason why they were unable to just send a wire. After a hasty back-and-forth of ideas, Ben came up with a plan that would gratify the requirements of the vendor while also allowing him to exact revenge on the vendor for causing him so much trouble.

Ben communicated to the title company that he was able to fulfil the merchant's request, and he stated that he would receive $2 million in actual money the next day. That nightfall, a guarded car delivered two million dollars to the location of the final organisation. The cash was then taken inside the title office by the armoured car half an hour before the closing took place. Ben had met the automobile outside the title company. After that, the title specialist took all of the money, totaled it, and made sure it added up to the correct total. Then, both the title agent and Ben began to rip off the paper sleeves that linked the cash together and set the loose bills on the closing table in a large mound. After this, they continued to place the cash in the safe.

The title company had the vendor sign, and then they transported him back to the room that kept the money he had requested when he had finished. What the buyer found was two million dollar dollars haphazardly stacked on a closing table. It was then up to him to evaluate it as well as transport it out of the end office and ultimately either store it in his bank or stuff it under his mattress. Both options were available to him.

Lessons in Education That Are Both Powerful and Profitable

(1) Ensure that your purchase agreement specifies that the assets to

the merchant can be in the form of cash, a clerk's cheque or a wire transfer.

 (2) Do not accept that a deal is going to complete until the vendor has marked the end papers and the cash has been distributed to the parties who are fitting into the arrangement.

With Wide-Open Eyes

Have you ever noticed that when you admire a certain automobile, it seems to drive past you all the more frequently at random intervals? This similar notion occurred to me when I realised how regularly I would go to a land get together and be one of a small group of women, if not the only woman in the room. This was the case even when there were other women present. I, too, observed how men predominated in the roles of speakers. Even in this day and age, I still come across seminars that only feature male speakers. My naturally inquisitive nature led me to ponder the next logical question, which was Why. Why is it that there are hardly no females participating in this activity? What are some of the possible explanations for the low number of female speakers?

My list of inquiries grew much longer when, a few months after that infamous instructive gathering, I made an effort to acquire capital for a real estate investment possibility involving condominiums. Every single one of the ladies I asked gave me the same response: "I'm not interested" or "I have to discuss this with my husband first," and in the end, they all responded, "I'm not interested." To my great good fortune, I had a significantly higher success rate when it came to interacting with males. Because of the current condition, I have an ever-growing list of questions to ask, and one of them is: Why aren't more girls investing in real estate?

My search for the answers to each address led me to a single direct connection that I kept coming back to, and that was the sex divide. The split is both intentional and unanticipated, and it can be perceived from a variety of perspectives, with the most commonly recognised one being the one that people consider to be analogous to the pay hole. Unfortunately, it starts long before you ever enter the workforce; you are inherently exposed to the class disparity at that point.

The typical lifespan

When my better half and I discuss what will take place in the event that one of us passes away, it is a running joke that we have, despite the fact that it is a quite morbid one. Finding stuff is one of my better half's weaknesses, while mine is anything having to do with being innovative. In point of fact, despite the fact that my significant other is younger than I am, it is highly likely that I will outlive him. According to the World Health Organisation, the average lifespan of a woman is somewhere between six and eight years. In the event that all goes according to plan, despite the fact that I will, as far as I can tell, continue to struggle with innovation, I will be able to make a living, and surviving off the earnings from the previous years will be of the utmost significance. This is true even if there is no doubt that this will occur.

According to the most recent data from the Bureau of Labour Statistics, the monthly average cost of necessities for an individual over the age of 60 is approximately $4,000 dollars. In the event that my partner passes away before me and we are the same age, I will need an additional $288,000 to $384,000 saved up in order to cover the cost of the expenses associated with my day-to-day living expenses. This is not to sound overly pessimistic.

Making the error of believing everything you read is a mistake.

Let's just be honest with one another. The overwhelming majority are complete idiots. You are in for a world of trouble if you start accepting advice from those dimwits, which is saying a lot, because they aren't that bright.

In today's world, I believe there is a true problem with TMI, which stands for an excessive amount of info. The internet is amazing because it provides enormous amounts of information and makes our life much easier overall. However, it can also make life more difficult in a variety of different ways. How would you know if what you are reading or hearing on the internet or from other people is true? You in no way do. You are going to need to learn how to translate data for yourself like never before in this day and age.

The first step in figuring out which statistics are the most important to pay attention to is to listen to the advice of people who are already successful in the same endeavours that you need to undertake. Because they are successful in their own endeavours, it is reasonable to assume that the vast majority of what they share with you has some degree of truth. Be wary, however, if you are participating in a discussion on an online forum in which there are essentially no controls over who is speaking or the content that is being discussed. Even the most ignorant and incompetent person can give the impression of being knowledgeable and authoritative online, even if the information they are providing is false and misleading.

Cars

Is it possible to bring cash in from vehicles? When you think about anything like this, you probably think about the market for classic cars or the market for exceptional vehicles.

You might also find methods to make money off of your vehicle by renting it out for special events like weddings. For example, you could rent it out as a limousine service.

The high initial cost of a vehicle leads many people to believe that purchasing one is a form of investment; yet, investments should result in a profit for their owners. A vehicle's value decreases over time and continues to get worse with each passing year.

Although the value of exceptional automobiles has increased over the course of the past 30 years, investing money in an exceptional engine is not a reliable way for acquiring a satisfactory return on investment. This is despite the fact that exceptional automobiles have been increasingly regarded.

If you need to invest resources into vehicles, you should certainly look for a vehicle that is a good fit for you in terms of both price and condition before making a purchase.

The majority of automobiles will never be an investment that will provide a profit because their value drops as soon as they are driven out of the showroom; nevertheless, exceptional automobiles increase in value over the course of their ownership.

Collectible status can be attained by automobiles that hold genuine historical significance, particularly if they are rare and/or beautiful.

The demand for handcrafted goods is reflected in the market for vehicles. It's a theory that appeals to your artistic sensibilities, right?

If you sell this property for a profit, you will be responsible for paying a capital increases fee because it is a substantial individual property.

You can purchase a vehicle that is brand new or almost brand new because you believe that it will become valuable at some point in the not too distant future; nevertheless, doing so is gambling.

Purchasing a vehicle can provide the following benefits:

• Class and individuality • The thrill of the drive • Your own sense of satisfaction

Purchasing a car comes with the following potential drawbacks:

Expenses in terms of money and time, lack of modern conveniences, upkeep, and loss in value

You are able to search for a model automobile on the internet.

Who, Rather Than How

The business visionary Russell Brunson is the source of one of the ideas that I gained, and that idea is "who, not how." When any of us tries our hand at something brand new, our natural inclination is to ask, "How?" as our first question. How are we going to get from point A to point B once we've arrived at guide A? The problem with that is that the answer to the question "how?" is almost always exceedingly murky and specialised. When something is confusing, a big number of people have a tendency to put it off, which ultimately results in them becoming stuck in their progression towards their final goal. This is the primary reason why people do not achieve their aims and make adequate progress towards their preparations for the future. They are asking questions that cannot be answered in this manner.

Tony Robbins is known for his repeated assertion that "Assuming you pose various inquiries, you'll find various solutions." Simply said, "who, not how" is the concept in question. Asking yourself, "How might I do this?" is the wrong question. Instead, you should be asking yourself, "Who can say for sure how to do this?" You have started the cycle by reading this book and learning my interaction on how to put together a profitable collection of lifestyle assets. I congratulate you on this achievement. Because you have been looking for us, you are currently going through this cycle. During the process of building your team, we will continue to ask supplemental "who" questions.

We are only now entering the most specialised phases of this cycle, the areas in which it is essential to have a solid understanding of the many industry expertise. When you start looking at properties, buying properties, overseeing them, setting them up, marketing them, and all of the other things that you will be doing in the real estate business, assembling the right people to work with you is an essential component of the interaction that will take place. You are not going to be able to complete this task on your own. There are certain people who are just outstanding at what they do. You will be the director of this ensemble, not the piano player; yet, you will have a plan to follow and a good knowledge of what should be done. yet, you will have both of these things.

The Big Three are comprised of three separate authorities whom I refer to collectively. In this particular cycle, each and every one of them carries a lot of weight. Your Realtor partners, your financing partners, and your management partners are the three most important colleagues that you really need to take some time and really meet and really sort out where they fit into your interaction. In all honesty, I will devote a whole section to them, but the three most important colleagues that you really need to take some time and really meet and really sort out where they fit into your interaction are your Realtor partners, your financing partners, and your Because a significant majority of your other coworkers will have come from references from these three, I find that it is customarily most beneficial to start with the Big Three at the outset.

Stock Markets According To A Technical Analysis

This is a technique for forecasting future market prices by analysing historical prices in conjunction with stock volume. This idea is the foundation for the majority of trading regulations, particularly those that govern volume and stock price.

Oscillators and indicators are the tools that are utilised in the process of technical analysis. These are the mathematical computations that are utilised in the process of determining the pace of the stock markets. The primary distinction between oscillators and indicators is in the fact that oscillators function only within a given range, but indicators do not have such restrictions. Bollinger bands, alligators, and moving averages are just a few examples of the types of indicators available. Oscillators come in many forms, but some of the most prevalent ones are commodities channel indices, moving average convergence divergence indices, and relative strength indices. Using technical analysis, investors may decide when it is the best time to join and exit a market, as well as when it is the best time to set stop-loss orders.

The only variables that are used as inputs for technical analysis are the stock price and the volume of the stock. This strategy makes the assumption that any other elements that affect the stock market are already incorporated in its price; as a result, it does not place an emphasis on how important it is to pay attention to these factors. The vast majority of technical analysts examine stock charts in order to identify patterns and trends that may be used to forecast the performance of a stock in the future. In order to determine the trends in the market, they use quantitative analysis in conjunction with behavioural economics.

The term "technical analysis" refers to a compilation of different approaches. The majority of these tactics concentrate on determining whether or not a particular stock or market trend will continue to exist. The tactics help to estimate when exactly the trend will stop continuing in the event that this is the case. Some of the analysts make use of trendlines and candlesticks, while others rely on chart patterns and boxes in their analysis. During the process of performing technical analysis, you could decide to employ many approaches simultaneously in order to improve the precision of the results. The best points for investors to enter and exit a trade are defined with the use of chart points.

This approach has been put into practise for a number of years. Dutch merchants were the ones who introduced it into use in the 17th century. The idea that market prices frequently include all of the information that a trader needs to make an investment is a fundamental tenet of the discipline of technical analysis.

Chart patterns are a subcategory of technical analysis that make it possible to discover points of support and resistance on a chart by making use of a collection of patterns. Typically, these patterns are representative of the psychological variables that are at play in the market. They assist you in making accurate forecasts regarding the movement of the market. For instance, a resistance area is shown on the chart by a pattern in the form of an ascending triangle. This indicates that whenever the prices break out of this range, there is a possibility that they will increase dramatically.

A group of technical indicators is an additional method of conducting technical analysis. These are statistical tools that give analysts the ability to apply mathematical formulas to the prices and volumes of stock. As a result of the ease with which they can be quantified, technical indicators have found a place in virtually all trading systems.

In spite of the wide variety of applications that may be found for technical analysis, there are a few limitations to the approach that you need to be aware of. The technical charts are highly susceptible to having their meanings misconstrued. This is most common when evaluating stock prices for companies that have minimal volume. When the fluctuation in stock price is too low, the periods that are utilised to compute moving averages may become excessively long, which can cause the analysis's results to become distorted. Another one of this method's distinct drawbacks is that as new techniques are implemented during the process, they each make a little impact on the prices that are now being offered on the market. For example, a strategy might forecast a bearish market; if traders believe this, they might be less likely to invest in the market, which would lead to a drop in stock prices.

Investing In Mutual Funds And Their Many Rewards

In 2018, an astounding amount of money, specifically $19 trillion, was put in mutual funds by investors all around the world. One of the advantages of investing in mutual funds, which is already familiar to us, is that it provides tremendous diversification. In the event that one of the companies in a mutual fund goes bankrupt or experiences other difficulties, the losses that are incurred by that company are likely going to be compensated for by gains made by the other companies in the fund. Therefore, the amount of risk that you are exposed to is quite low. Keep in mind that there is always a risk to the entire system. Even if you invest in a mutual fund, there is still a possibility that you will not be protected from systemic risk because a decline in the economy would also result in a decline in the value of mutual funds. On the other hand, it reduces risks that are not systemic.

Investing in mutual funds gives you the ability to gain diversified exposure to a wide number of firms while yet allowing you the convenience of making investments of a more modest scale. There is a minimum amount of money that must be invested in many different mutual funds. Some investment funds may demand a minimum investment of $500, while others may require an investment of up to $5,000. The minimum amount required to invest may vary from fund to fund. It is important to keep this in mind, however as we will see in the following section, exchange traded funds are able to sidestep this kind of restriction. As a result, these funds provide a superior option for many investors seeking the same benefits.

Mutual funds are a popular choice among investors since they are a sort of passive investing. That is to say, when you invest in mutual funds, you are not going to have any active role to play other than determining whether or not you want to get out of the fund or acquire more shares of the fund's stock. There is no need for you to educate yourself on the principles of the organisation or anything similar to that. Because if you are trying to establish a self-managed portfolio, you might be highly interested in the idea of examining companies and stock selection, most readers are not going to be interested in this strategy because it focuses on stock picking rather than investigating companies. When it comes to mutual funds, that sort of thing just does not occur.

Various funds seek to achieve various objectives with their investments. One of the reasons why so many investors are drawn to mutual funds is because of this. Therefore, if you are interested in rapid expansion, you might look for a mutual fund that was established solely for the goal of achieving that objective. You could also look for investments that offer a high dividend yield. In addition, there is the option of investing in value stock through mutual funds. You have the option of investing in mutual funds that are designed to safeguard your capital, as well as other mutual funds that are geared to provide significant growth.

When you invest in a mutual fund, the management of the fund itself is handled by a qualified fund manager on your behalf. Therefore, with the objectives of the fund in mind, the management of the fund is going to make purchases and sales of shares of stock in companies that they believe will help maintain a high level of performance for the fund. In most cases, the objective is to achieve a higher value than some market index. You will know that you have a successful investment, for instance, if you are making investments and those investments are performing better than the S&P 500. This may be difficult to accomplish for an average investor, but the concept of a professional fund manager has actually been met with some degree of resistance in recent years. The question of whether or not a money manager genuinely delivers a considerable benefit, or even whether they provide any benefit at all, is at the centre of the debate that has sparked the issue. Because of the high financial toll it exacts, the presence of the fund manager is not an unimportant factor. The numerous fees that you are required to pay in order to maintain your investment in the mutual fund cover the costs associated with this endeavour.

investine ic operant tor of y
store a finaait. ore flows
salt are performers or trm
the 38t tes ror be difficult to
ac with ur an divchs tn
arre in a rot resurn. And
tub mard ne

Which Investment Portfolio Is Best Suited To Your Needs?

The body of work produced by an artist resembles the courting behaviour of a peacock; it is vibrant, interesting, and intricate.

Does this imply that the portfolio of a passive investor must always have the same structure? Because we are slackers who invest, as long as it's up to us, the answer is no. We are investors who place a high value on clarity.

Before even beginning to consider the possibility of putting together a portfolio, there are two choices that need to be made:

Evaluation of your capacity to deal with uncertain circumstances - this will be figured out very soon.

Conduct research on the many investment possibilities available to you. There are a great deal of ETFs currently available. At the conclusion of this book, you will be aware of the proper way to carry out these steps.

Investing in particular industries, such as healthcare or aviation, or in large-scale retailers like Walmart is now accessible thanks to exchange-traded funds (ETFs) that monitor indices. There is no need to speculate as to whether business will come out with a major virus cure, a faster aeroplane, or a new shopping technology first. You are able to make an investment in an entire market and all of the companies that make up that market by purchasing securities that invest in either many or all of the companies that make up that market. For instance, you have the option of investing in exchange-traded funds that represent the entirety of the retail and pharmaceutical industries in the United States. A celebration of medicines and toilet paper might be part of your investment portfolio.

BUT! If you haven't worked out what I'm trying to tell you yet, the strategy that I'm trying to offer to you will not promote any favouritism towards any particular industry, stock, or country. I find it more prudent to invest in the entire market because there is no reason to suppose that you have information that the market does not have. In other words, if something is bringing in money for you, don't mess with it!

An investor who makes the decision to put all of their money into stocks has the option of putting their money into a portfolio that follows a worldwide stock index (like the American Vanguard VT). Investing in just one of those can surely provide enough diversity, and if you want something that has a global reach, it's the same as owning hundreds of different companies.

Another example that you are already familiar with is purchasing the S&P 500 index fund, which is analogous to purchasing shares in 500 prosperous companies. These companies are all incorporated in the United States of America, but they sell their goods and services to millions of customers in other countries. I don't know how you feel about that, but I think that would be very exciting.

Bonds constitute the portion of a portfolio that holds the least amount of interest.

Your portfolio's bonds are exceedingly boring and offer no return on investment. Imagine something in your life that was incredibly tedious, such as maths lesson, a date you went on, or a movie you absolutely despised. That's a bond. ETFs that track bond indices can be used by a sloppy investor who wants to supplement his investing portfolio with items that are less volatile than equities. These bond indices are spread out over multiple redemption dates and by several issuers. When an investor purchases the Vanguard Total Bond ETF (ticker symbol: BND), they will get the impression that they are purchasing a single share that is comprised of a wide variety of American bonds. You shouldn't let the idea throw you for a loop:

This ETF will hold a total of 27% bonds, 27% of which will have a redemption duration of between one and three years.

29% of them will be subject to a redemption period of between three and five years.

15% will have a redemption time that ranges from twenty to thirty years.

An exchange-traded fund (ETF) that represents multiple different kinds of bonds is a great choice for investors (lazy ones) who do not like to spend a lot of time investigating the various bond products and all of their merits and downsides. You can expect a return from these assets that is not as great as you would get from an equity ETF, but the volatility is significantly lower than that of an equity ETF. The passive investor can get a good night's sleep thanks to exchange-traded bond funds (ETFs).

The following is a list of Stephen's expenditures:

The cost of lunch at school is currently $5.50 per day. (The price of the school lunch increased by 50 cents, but Stephen never paid any attention to the price change, therefore he never informed his parents that the price had changed.)

$2.50 every day for an after-school snack (Stephen bought the special from the pizza every day because his friend Bryan did, and because of that, Stephen did the same). Two pieces of pizza and a Coke cost a total of $2.50. Stephen just ate one of the pieces and then threw the other one away. That indicates that Stephen squandered his snack after school and spent money on something that he threw away on a daily basis.)

And now it is time to go on to the third stage, which is the list that the majority of people who budget ignore. Stephen was all set to make a list of the things that he ardently wished for himself.

What Stephen wished for was a brand-new pair of Vans trainers.

Another game for the Xbox

A MP3 player that is portable.

"Wow," Stephen thought to himself, "I'll never be able to acquire that amazing stuff." He came to the conclusion that he was squandering his money on gum, baseball cards, and other objects of low value because the thing that he truly desired was so expensive that he did not believe he would ever be able to purchase it. Without a budget, he would have blown all of his money on things that were only good for the short term instead of working towards his long-term objectives.

Take a look at what Stephen has done with the money he has available. First, he discussed the matter with his parents the fact that the price of a school lunch had increased. They gave him an additional fifty cents on a daily basis. Following that, he refrained from purchasing the pizza special. Instead, he shelled out $1.50 for a single slice and fetched an additional glass of juice from his house. As a result of Stephen's improvements, he was able to save $7.50 per week, and their friendship has not been severed.

Stephen started to direct his attention to the things that would bring him the most fulfilment. After getting his parents' approval, he searched eBay until he located an old MP3 player selling for a price that was extremely affordable. In addition to this, Stephen informed everyone he knew about the Xbox game he desired and asked if they had any ideas as to where he could purchase it at a reduced price. Within the span of a week, a young lady by the name of Judy proposed that they trade her game for a few CDs and the sum of $14.00 in cash.

Your First Entry Into The Market

It is time to start putting your new information to use since now that you hopefully have a clear grasp of just what all the components are that go into producing a solid options trade, it is time to get started trading using your newfound knowledge. This is a process that consists of two parts: the first part, which is coming up with the appropriate plan, and the second part, which is carrying out that plan in the appropriate manner.

Develop a strategy.

Before you can start engaging in profitable trading, the first thing you are going to need to do is give some thought to the process of developing your own individual trading strategy. This plan will have various components that are specific to you, and moving forward without taking the time to build your own plan is a solid way to put an end to your career in options trading before it even gets started.

To begin, take an inventory of your skills: When it comes to ensuring that you have the appropriate options trading strategy, the first thing you are going to want to do is take a look at your overall skill level and familiarity with trading in general, if not options trading specifically. This is going to be the first step that you are going to want to take in order to ensure that you have the appropriate options trading plan. There is a natural tendency among many rookie traders of options to exaggerate their level of expertise early on, but doing so will do nothing but slow you down in the long term. Be truthful with yourself and make an accurate list of your strengths and limitations. To be more specific, you need to have a crystal clear sense of the likelihood that you will deviate from your plan in order to act in accordance with your feelings. This is a common mistake, and if you are aware of it being one of your tendencies, you will need to devise a strategy to work around it.

Think about other obstacles: When it comes to selecting what strategy or method works for you, it will be vital to take into consideration any other potential obstacles that you might need to overcome in order to attain the level of success that you are wanting to achieve. These obstacles could include things like time constraints, financial constraints, or interpersonal conflicts. These kinds of obstacles can take many forms, ranging from a deficiency in finances or planning to an issue that is both more complex and more deeply personal. The point is that anything outside of the typical market inconsistencies that prohibit options trading from being purely successful should be accounted for to guarantee that your success rate remains as high as possible. This will ensure that your success rate remains as high as feasible.

Think about the degree of danger that is acceptable to you: When it comes to determining how much risk is appropriate for you, the first thing you are going to want to do is decide how much money you are going to be able to put into investments overall. After that, you can move on to determining how much risk you are comfortable taking. If you have never put any money into the stock market previously, then this investing budget might be considered to be your portfolio. When it comes to trading, a good rule of thumb is to never invest more than 5 percent of your total into any one deal. This reduces the risk of losing a significant amount of money in a single transaction. In addition, you are going to want to establish whether or not the deal is worth the effort by making certain that it is going to pay out at least three hundred percent when compared with the initial expenditure.

When it comes to any options trade, you can easily calculate the risk-to-reward ratio by simply taking the amount of expected profit and dividing it by the amount of the investment. This gives you the risk per unit of potential return. If the outcome is larger than or equal to three, the deal may be profitable and hence worth your effort if it does so. However, it is essential to keep in mind that the return will only occur if the trade works in your favour, which can be established by discovering your own degree of tolerance when it comes to the risk of investment.

The ratio of the amount of time you have available to work on investing to the amount of possible returns you are looking for is one way to determine your own personal risk tolerance level.

Another method for determining your risk tolerance level is to ask yourself how much money you hope to make from your investments. If you want to make more than a moderate amount of money from trading options, you are going to have to be willing to take on a higher level of risk. This follows from the fact that the less time you are willing to spend trading options, the higher level of risk you are going to have to be willing to accept.

Complete your assignments: Each and every day in the hours before the market opens, you need to plan on being in front of some kind of screen, learning about everything that occurred while you were asleep and choosing how you think it is going to effect the markets you are most interested in. If you don't do this, you could miss out on opportunities to make money. This necessitates looking at a variety of different markets, such as those overseas, the premarket forecast, and index futures, to name just a few, in order to get a sense of how the market is likely to behave after the trading session has gotten off to a proper start and the day has fully begun.

You will also want to make sure that you are always informed of any forthcoming due dates for income data that has to be reported, since these deadlines will always disrupt the market in question in some way or another. There are four times a year when businesses are required to report their earnings in relation to their expectations, and the findings almost always have the potential to have a significant impact on the market. Waiting until the flurry of panic trading has subsided and entering the market after things begin to stabilise is the best course of action in these situations; however, one should not wait so long that there is no longer an opportunity to make a profit by doing so.

Make a decision regarding an exit strategy: No matter what plan or approach you ultimately decide to go with, it is critical to have a crystal clear understanding of what constitutes an acceptable degree of profit or loss for you, and to devise a solid exit strategy in accordance with that definition. Waiting for an underlying stock to rebound before exercising your option or walking away is seldom going to end in your favour, and it can develop to a terrible habit of holding on to subpar deals, which could potentially cost you a lot of money over the long term. The results are rarely going to end in your favour. The best exit strategy for you will differ depending on how much risk you are willing to take, how many trades you intend to make each day, and how comfortable you are with micromanaging your investments. Whatever the case may be, the time at which you decide to get out of a terrible trade should be consistent throughout all of your other trades.

To begin developing an efficient exit plan, the first step is to determine where the optimal position is to place a limit order, also known as a stop loss. When you buy an option, you will be given the opportunity to place an automated order known as a stop loss. This order will specify the price at which you want the option to be sold on its own. You can use it to limit the amount of money you lose in the event that a trade unexpectedly moves in the other direction of what you had hoped it would. You should avoid placing stop losses on options that are particularly volatile because it is possible that their value will fluctuate too much for them to be truly useful in this situation.

Stop orders are helpful if you are the writer as well as the holder because they can be used to ensure that further options are purchased if the price climbs instead. This is because stop orders can be used to ensure that additional options are purchased if the price rises. You might also find it helpful to utilise a secondary stop order, which is an order that sells the asset in question if the price reaches a certain secondary amount. This value is referred to as the price goal, and it is the sum that you can anticipate making from the trade in question with the greatest degree of certainty. When you reach your price objective, you should liquidate fifty percent of your total holdings and bring the first stop point up to the current level. You should do this as soon as possible. This raises the possibility for your profits while also lowering the total risk you take on.

Take, as an illustration, the scenario in which you own two options, the sum of which is 200 shares of a stock that is currently valued at $20. In order to limit the amount of money you stand to lose, you would place a stop loss order at

$19.75. If the stock then reaches your price target of $30, the best course of action is to sell 100 shares to ensure that you see some profit from your price target before hanging on to the remaining shares and setting a new stop loss of $30. If the stock does not hit your price target, the next best course of action is to hold on to the remaining shares and set a new stop loss of $30. In this manner, you will be certain to realise the profits associated with your earlier price goal, while at the same time leaving yourself open to the possibility of additional profits under the assumption that the upward trend in the underlying stock continues.

Where Can I Locate Information Regarding Microcap And Penny Stock Companies?

This is a difficult topic to answer because one of the drawbacks of investing in penny stocks is how difficult it may be to obtain information on those stocks. However, simply because it may be challenging does not mean that it is completely impossible, and there are surely a few things that you may do in order to obtain the information that you require. Keep in mind that you should stay away from a certain penny stock if you have trouble finding information about it or if there is nothing positive to report about it. The less information that is disclosed, the greater the possibility that it is a con. When looking for a solid firm to invest in, transparency is definitely something that should be sought after as a desirable quality.

To begin, it is in your best interest to inquire with the company as to whether or not it is in fact registered with the SEC and whether or not it submits the required reports to the SEC. Imagine that a corporation is not required to comply with this regulation because it is too small. If this is the case, one option available to you is to contact the state authorities in your area in order to obtain the information you require. You can also explore contacting the company management and brokers who have suggested that you invest in the firm. If you know somebody who has previously invested in the company, you should inquire with them about how well it is doing. However, keep in mind that you need to exercise caution and common sense with regard to the information you obtain. You have to think about whether or not the company's management has the right kind of experience to carry out the business plan that it promotes. This indicates that you should have a solid understanding of the proper procedures for running a corporation. Although it would appear to be self-evident, the vast majority of individuals are not familiar with that bit of general information. It is possible that you will need to assess whether or not the company have the appropriate resources or any kind of competitive edge that demonstrates any kind of potential for success. In conclusion, use caution while perusing the webpage of the organisation. Even something as simple as examining the product's quality and appearance can provide a decent indication of how current it is with regard to the ever-evolving digital world. You might also think about looking up information on the company on websites that are associated with the OTC market.

As a result of the need that many corporations have to file their reports with the SEC, information is available from that organisation. This indicates that you may utilise the EDGAR database of the SEC to find which firm files at the SEC itself (in the event that you are unable to make contact with management, you can always check there), and that you can obtain the reports that the company has sent in to file. If, on the other hand, a corporation files its reports with the SEC but does not place them on EDGAR, you can contact the SEC through its online form or send an email to the public information office to obtain the information you require.

You can also find the information by contacting the state agency that regulates securities in your area. This is particularly relevant in the event that you have trouble obtaining the information of the microcap firm directly from the company, your broker, or even the SEC. As you can see, you do have a few choices and locations to turn to in order to obtain the information that you are seeking. If you call the state securities regulator, you will be able to determine whether or not the company has been given the legal go-ahead to sell securities in your state and whether or not they have been cleared of any legal violations. Because the majority of traders will not go to such lengths in their efforts to obtain the information that is necessary, this is a foolproof method for avoiding the vast majority of the cons and cons that are currently available. But there is a cost associated with sloth, and there is also a cost associated with wisdom. Take your time and make sure you have complete faith in the business before you even consider bringing any kind of financial transaction near them.

In addition to that, you can verify with other government regulators. For instance, the Securities and Exchange Commission does not require a lot of corporations, such as certain banks, to submit reports to them. However, the financial information held by the banks or corporations in question must have been kept up to date and filed with their respective banking regulators. In addition, many of the governing bodies may be accessed relatively easily online. Therefore, you are able to find what you require without having to leave the convenience of your own home.

Reference books, websites, and even corporate databases are all frequent places to look for answers to research questions. It might not be a bad idea to pay a visit to the library at your local public institution, as well as the library at the closest business or law school. There are a lot of reference materials that happen to include information that you might require about firms, particularly the company that you will be interested in. You can find all of this information in the references that you locate. In addition, you have the ability to access commercial databases, which may contain a great deal more information on a company's history, products and services, management, revenues, and can even go as far as the credit ratings, which are essential for seeing how a firm manages its debt. Once more, conducting adequate research frequently necessitates going beyond the call of duty. This is undoubtedly a wise example, however it is better to obtain all of the necessary facts now rather than regretting it later and suffering a significant loss. When you use a commercial database, there is opportunity for consultation, and there is a possibility that you will receive a more expert view on how the companies are doing. This is because the SEC is not allowed to support or recommend any sort of business. In light of the legal requirement that the SEC maintain its objectivity at all times, a novice could do well, in spite of the fact that they have access to the required reports, to begin consulting with experts in the commercial database.

This Is All Very Exciting News, But What Does Any Of This Have To Do With Cryptocurrency?

When it comes to the expansion of metaverse ecosystems as a whole, I would suggest that the most straightforward response is that certain blockchain-based gaming protocols have the potential to be regarded as the genuine pioneering forces. Even though major technology companies like Meta and Microsoft have just recently set their claims to the metaverse, the fact of the matter is that some early visual hints of the metaverse can already be seen in popular online games like Minecraft, Second Life, and even RuneScape. This is because Minecraft was one of the first games to implement a sandbox-style environment in which players could build their own virtual worlds.

The NFTs, Gaming, and the Emergence of the Metaverse

The combination of these three key aspects, in my opinion, provides us with a clearer glimpse into what the most true form of the metaverse will look like when it is fully realised. The term "metaverse" can be used to describe anything that is more analogous to an online arena where decentralised finance (DeFi) reigns supreme as well as a virtual world that merges gaming, augmented reality, non-fungible tokens (NFTs), cryptocurrencies, and blockchain technology.

Many people, when they hear the term "NFT," their minds immediately jump to thoughts of pixelated treasures, odd-looking ape figures, and digital artworks, all of which are linked to what appears to be an excessive amount of money. NFTs are now able to experiment with their built-in functions and make use of their particular in-game utilities thanks to the advent of virtual realities and gaming spheres, which have eventually widened the playing field for NFTs. This is primarily due to the fact that apart from the manic digital art frenzy that NFTs have been caught up in, the architecture inherent in an NFT offers the bearer a digital certificate of verifiable ownership over an object in the virtual sphere. This is true even though NFTs have been swept up in the manic digital art frenzy.

If we accept the premise that the metaverse is an enhanced parallel representation of the actual world, then we may also consider it to be an extension of that universe. NFTs allow holders to use and leverage their assets, whether it be a valuable crypto punk or board ape avatar, a plot of digital real estate, or an in-game item inside the metaverse environment. This is analogous to what happens with ownership contracts in the real world. NFTs and the metaverse will most certainly continue to develop in tandem with one another and will most likely continue to develop in a manner that is relatively akin to their future progress. This is ultimately the case due to the fact that NFT-based metaverses that combine assets and blockchain into their underlying technology have the potential to bring in an altogether new economic framework as well as a forward-thinking financial paradigm inside their own ecosystems.

Even though metaverse-like environments have been present in

105

massively multiplayer online games for quite some time now, the implementation of blockchain technology, non-fungible tokens (NFTs), digital assets, and virtual reality in this industry is not only drastically changing who can participate in and enter these environments, but it is also demonstrating the real-world market value of the assets, the interactions, and the experiences earned in the digital realms of blockchain games.

Putting together NFTs

NFTs, also known as non-fictional things, are anything else that may be bought or sold in the Metaverse. This includes artwork, avatars, products, buildings, and even wearables. Anything that can be designed on a computer and saved there can be uploaded to the Metaverse. You just need some essential design abilities to get started.

On websites such as Skillshare and udemy, you can take courses to improve your design talents.

You can acquire the skills necessary to produce a wide variety of items, and then upload them to the Metaverse to be sold. You can even design avatars or structures specifically for individual users.

The stocks of Metaverse

If you are interested in this sector of the economy, you may invest in a number of different Metaverse stocks. Amazon, Microsoft, Facebook, Apple, and a number of other companies are among the most successful ones.

Providers of the Metaverse

I suggest that you look at metaverse services if you aren't too keen on the stocks but are more interested in the services itself. People want to enter the Metaverse, and they want to make their name known within the Metaverse. However, in order to do either of those things, they are going to require some assistance, such as assistance in developing an avatar that resembles them or assistance in developing a house. All of it needs to be designed, and you can turn it into a business by hosting your services on a platform such as Fiverr.

You have the option of either purchasing these services and then reselling them, or of learning how to make them and then selling them directly on Fiverr, Upwork, or one of the other platforms.

People are spending money on shoes, skins, avatars, and other non-functional items (NFTs) so that they can walk around the Metaverse looking good. If you are a designer, or even if you only have the ability to learn some fundamental design abilities, there is a big opportunity for you.

Method Three: Working Partial Hours The Paperboy

Becoming a part-time paperboy is yet another fantastic option to get started making money on your own. I had a lot of fun engaging in activities like this while I was at my parents' house for the holidays. In addition to that, it is a wonderful chance to develop closer relationships with those who live nearby.

Those who walk from home to home delivering newspapers are known as "paperboys." The term "newspaper carrier" refers to individuals that either drive a van, ride bicycles, or walk in order to deliver newspapers. Paperboys typically work a variety of shifts, including nights, mornings, or weekends, and are required to follow a set route that is specified by the newspaper industry.

Place an advertisement in the paper that serves your area. At local newspapers, prospective paper carriers commonly fill out registration forms, which may be paper-based or available online. Please ensure that your personal contact information is correct before submitting the application. A telephone recruitment line is made available by some newspapers, and anyone looking for work can use this line to send their applications. In addition to this, visit the website of the newspaper and search for the telephone number in order to exclude any more possibilities.

Conduct a search on internet job boards for openings that are local to you. Conduct a search on the internet for newspapers that are sold in the immediate area. Call the publications and ask in a respectful manner if they are currently accepting applications. In the event that you are not selected for employment, it is in your best interest to inquire about the possibility of having your information kept on file in the event that another vacancy opens up.

Look through the classified ads that are published in your local paper. When employment opportunities for paperboys become available, the newspaper may post them on the website in order to make use of a cost-effective recruitment strategy.

Ensure that you promptly respond to any phone calls or emails related to your application that you get from a publication. Maintain a professional demeanour and get ready to take part in an interview, whether it be over the phone or in person. Think ahead about the questions that an employer might ask you so that you can come up with good answers and be ready for the interview. If you are under the age of 18, you need to acquire permission from your parents. If you are ever unclear about anything, you should ask your parents for assistance. My father got me my first work as a newspaper carrier by talking to some of his acquaintances, and it turned out to be one of the most enjoyable jobs I've ever had. I had a great time travelling and meeting new people, and along the way, a few customers were kind enough to tip me a few extra cents as I was making my regular deliveries.

Your Most Important Challenger

We are not going to talk about the most significant challenge you face when it comes to investing and life in general. You are your own adversary. There is no other person who will stand in your way of having success with investments as much as you will. Earlier, we had a discussion on mentality. If you do not cultivate the right mentality for investing, it is quite unlikely that you will ever begin the endeavour, let alone be successful at it. As you make investments, you should be aware that there are some outcomes that will not be in your favour. Things might still go wrong even if you do all of the research and perform the tasks in the way that they are meant to be done. You must not let this deter you in any way. Gain wisdom from your past errors, but also maintain the perseverance to keep going forward.

When it comes to investments, there are a lot of mistakes that people make as they go along. Understanding some of the most common errors will help you avoid being your own worst enemy, despite the fact that there is no way to completely eliminate the possibility of making mistakes. When getting started in the world of investing, there are a few things you definitely want to stay away from doing.

a lack of comprehension of either the firm or the investment. A lot of people put their money into companies just because they've heard stories about how successful certain companies are, even when they haven't done any study on the companies themselves. They are, in all intents and purposes, going into it blind and hoping for the best. Warren Buffett, the most successful investor in the history of the world, has cautioned investors not to put their money into businesses whose business models they do not fully comprehend.

It's important to keep your concentration on the task at hand and not get attached to a particular firm. It is easy to forget why you invested in a firm in the first place when that company begins to generate profits for its shareholders. You may find yourself falling so deeply in love with the firm that you will be unable to see many of the issues that arise. If you choose to ignore what is happening in front of your eyes, you can miss the fact that the company is failing right in front of your eyes. Never lose sight of the fact that this is being done for the sake of business and profit. Once a firm is no longer producing profits for you, it is time to consider selling it.

It is true that patience is a virtue, and that a lack of it can be harmful. To achieve any kind of success in life over the long term, you will need to go forward in a methodical and consistent manner. This includes making financial investments. Because there will be numerous highs and lows, you really have to have an attitude that is highly disciplined. You need to keep your focus and be aware that making decisions on the spur of the moment will set you back in terms of your potential for future financial success.

Even for seasoned traders, trying to predict when the market will move may be an extremely challenging endeavour. If you are inexperienced, you should not even think of doing it.

Transaction fees and short-term tax rates might eat away at earnings if there is a lot of rapid turnover throughout an investment or if there is an excessive amount of cash collection. After deducting all of the fees, there is a chance that you will come out ahead, or at the very least, break even. In addition, you run the risk of missing out on certain potential long-term benefits. This concept is closely related to the timing of the market as well as exercising patience.

Investors make a mistake when they wait for their investments to equal out. This indicates that you are holding on to an investment that is losing value in the hopes that it will increase in value again so that you can sell it for at least what it is currently worth. Even if this does take place, the odds are that you will still end up losing in two different ways. To begin, there is always a risk that the value of the investment will continue to decline and eventually reach zero.

Second, by not moving your money to a different investment, you run the risk of missing out on opportunities that could turn out to be profitable.

When you diversify your investments, you reduce the risk of suffering excessive financial loss while increasing your chances of coming out ahead overall. A lot of people don't do this and instead count on one or two items to get them to a point where they are financially independent. For instance, some of the investments in your portfolio might not be performing as well as others, but overall, it might be doing rather well. If you are not an experienced investor, you should adhere strictly to the notion of diversification.

People let their feelings to dictate their behaviour. If you invest for a significant amount of time, you will experience both incredible highs and devastating lows.

This is something you need to know going into it. You are going to experience a wide range of feelings as a result of this. Do not give in to the power that these feelings hold over you. For instance, do not enter into any investment without first doing your homework simply because the potential piques your interest, and do not sell an investment without first considering all of your options simply because you are anxious about it. Maintain command of your feelings and keep them under check.

In the end, you will wind up being your most formidable adversary. Even though there is always going to be some degree of risk associated with investing, you still need to do your homework and go forward in a way that is most beneficial to you. Put yourself to the test and strive to improve your investing skills constantly.

As you get started on a career in investing, I think it's important for you to get acquainted with the competitors you'll be up against. Beyond these four, there are going to be further possibilities. It is my hope that these challenges will not discourage you from pursuing a career as a successful investor. I must emphasise once more that my goal here is not to make you into Warren Buffett. It would be fantastic if you used this book as a springboard to become the next great global investor, and if that happens, you would have started with this book. Be aware, however, that you will face numerous challenges along the path that will require you to persevere and refocus your efforts. The more money you put in, the more difficult the problems you'll have to solve. Recognise them, educate yourself on them, and respect them, but do not allow yourself to be manipulated by them.

What exactly is meant by the term "Bitcoin Cash"?

A small but sizable portion of the Bitcoin community initiated a hard fork on August 1, which resulted in the creation of a new cryptocurrency known as Bitcoin Cash (abbreviated as BCC or BCH on exchanges). This fork led to the creation of Bitcoin Cash. The fork will result in larger block sizes and faster transaction speeds, both of which will lead to a reduction in the costs associated with conducting transactions. The original size of a Bitcoin block was 1 megabyte, however it has since been increased all the way up to 8 megabytes. The scaling problems that Bitcoin is now having prompted the creation of this split in order to find a solution.

Since Bitcoin Cash is considered to be the more advanced cryptocurrency in terms of technology, why wouldn't I invest in that instead?

Since we are, to tell you the truth, still in the preliminary stages, it is a question that is difficult to respond to. At the time of this writing, the split has been in effect for a little over a month, and Bitcoin Cash has already experienced major price shifts. The level of liquidity is far lower than that of Bitcoin, which makes large-scale sales difficult, and the repercussions of adoption in the real world are not yet known. If you are just starting out in the world of finance, you should keep a watch on Bitcoin Cash. Bitcoin, on the other hand, continues to be the most widely used cryptocurrency despite the fact that its network effects are not as potent as they once were.

In terms of the price of Bitcoin on the market, the Bitcoin Cash split that took place on August 1 initially caused a decline in the price of Bitcoin, but by the end of August, it had climbed to an all-time high. The value of Bitcoin Cash had an initial drop, followed by a rise, and then a resetting to approximately $550.

If you bought Bitcoin after the 1st of August 2017, you should view Bitcoin

Cash as a completely separate currency from Bitcoin. Any transaction that takes place in Bitcoin that also takes place in Bitcoin Cash will not be replicated. If you wish to acquire Bitcoin, you should search for the code BTC on exchanges. If you purchased Bitcoin prior to the 1st of August, you might be able to purchase Bitcoin Cash at the same price as Bitcoin.

Ethereum, Version 2.2.2

In spite of the fact that Ethereum and Bitcoin are both examples of distributed ledger technologies (DLTs), the Ethereum network was developed specifically to facilitate the creation, publication, monetization, and consumption of decentralised applications (dApps). Ether (ETH), the platform's native currency, was designed to function as a form of payment when it was first introduced.

In September of 2021, Ether was the second most widely used virtual currency, trailing only Bitcoin in popularity. The production of ETH also makes use of a process known as proof-of-work. In contrast to Bitcoin, however, there is no cap placed on the total amount of ETH that can be produced.

The proliferation of initial coin offerings can be partially attributed to Ethereum'sblockchain technology, which is used by a number of different ICOs. Non-fungible tokens, also known as NFTs, are digital representations of artwork or collectibles that are linked to a blockchain and are produced one-of-a-kind. The rise in popularity of NFTs may be directly attributed to Ethereum.

What exactly is the process of creation, and how does it function?

One day, the Canadian software developer VitalikButerin, who has Russian background, was thinking about the problems with Bitcoin. In the end, he came to the conclusion that the use of Bitcoin (and cryptocurrencies in general) as a form of payment was only a small portion of what it could potentially be.

After becoming aware of the benefits of Blockchain, which cannot be altered by third parties, he developed a novel concept that he calls smart contracts. Since it is possible for such a network to store virtually any kind of information,

Buterin decided to create his very own blockchain and call it Ethereum.

Ethereum's distributed ledger, or blockchain, is quite similar to Bitcoin's, with the key difference being that Ethereum'sblockchain may be used for more than just transactions.

Since each new block on Ethereum'sblockchain is generated on the network within 15 seconds rather than 10 minutes, Ethereum'sblockchain has a significant advantage over Bitcoin'sblockchain. On the other hand, in my opinion, one of the most significant advantages of Ethereum'sblockchain is the fact that its creator is a real-life, flesh-and-blood individual. VitalikButerin is dedicated to the sustained development of his platform and has demonstrated this dedication by participating in a number of cryptocurrency conferences, exchanging ideas, and establishing bank consortiums, among other activities.

Companies In The Role Of Investors

As was noted earlier, businesses will invest their surplus cash in the hopes of increasing their overall profitability over the course of their operations. They have the option of investing in companies that are not in any way connected to their core business in order to generate returns or to eventually acquire control of the target company. It is acceptable for your company to make investments in other businesses; however, the very last thing you want is for your firm to consent to investments in place of genuine payment for the services and items it provides.

Regarding Intangible Assets

When it comes to earning sales and obtaining an advantage over the other businesses in your industry, soft assets, also known as intangible assets, are just as important as their physical counterparts. They consist of copyrights, patents, trademarks, brand names, and franchises, in addition to the goodwill acquired via the purchase of other businesses. Although it can be difficult, it is necessary to assign a monetary value to intangible assets.

How to Put a Price on Something That Can't Be Touched

In order to assign a value to soft assets, it is necessary to be familiar with both their current carrying value and the elements that make up their makeup. You also need to bear in mind the origin of the goodwill, whether it be patents, acquisitions, or something else. If you are looking at the accounting for intangible assets, you should be extremely sceptical when it comes to goodwill accounts that are particularly large.

When it comes to a firm and its acquisition plans, simplicity is what you desire, especially in situations when there are a lot of intangibles and goodwill to take into consideration. If you decide to put your money into a firm that has aggressive business practises when it comes to mergers and acquisitions, then you are asking for a headache that will never go away.

The Conventional Wisdom Regarding Investments and Intangible Assets

When valuing a corporation using the traditional method, it is recommended that intangible assets be ignored because there is no real value in them. When one firm acquires another for a price that is significantly higher than what they ought to have to pay, this may be the case. When evaluating a company, however, thanks to advancements in technology and the present climate of marketing, factors such as brand equity and intellectual capital may and should be taken into account. Brilliant branding tactics are responsible, in no small part, for the majority of the success enjoyed by today's most prosperous businesses. If you have any doubts about this, try pouring a bottle of Coca-Cola into a bottle labelled with a generic name, and then seeing how many of those bottles you can sell. If you don't establish a brand that people recognise, can relate to, and have faith in, you will never achieve the level of success that Coca-Cola has.

Accountable obligations

Current obligations and long term liabilities are the two categories that make up the category of liabilities.

Liabilities that are Current

When it comes to present liabilities, the payment for them is expected within the next year at the most. Let's take a look at some significant liabilities that should be kept in mind while we go over the books.

Payables include any and all sums of money that are owing to third parties as payment for goods and services that were obtained. As soon as a monetary payment is received, this liability is immediately discharged. The majority of businesses keep track of the ongoing balance of their current accounts payable, in addition to other records of a similar nature like their interest payable. When the payment for the patent is made in advance in the form of a deposit, then the portion of the payment that has not yet been earned is classified as a liability. This occurs whenever the payment is made.

In the realm of corporate finance, there has been a significant decline in the amount of emphasis placed on making it a goal to eliminate all short-term obligations. The reason for this is that certain businesses are able to conduct their day-to-day business operations utilising OPM, which stands for "other people's money." Accounts payable almost often include a grace period of thirty days before the payment is due, and this must be complied with. To put it another way, we are talking about "free money." The fact that the company will need very little in the way of equity capital requirements in order to keep the business going results in an extremely high return on the equity that was spent.

Keeping this in mind, the only changes in the status of your current liabilities that require your attention are those that are significant. The current liabilities are not a cause for alarm. They have the potential to assist the organisation in achieving significant profits while simultaneously reducing risk and costs.

Putting Money Into a Neighbourhood Enterprise

Just the year before last, I was perusing a blog that discussed the benefits of investing in local companies. I had the impression that this was going to be an article about how large corporations were beginning to invest in local businesses; however, it turned out to be about how regular people are establishing lines of communication with local businesses in order to offer them support and assistance. This is especially true for new businesses, which are typically in the process of expanding in order to reach the critical mass of customers necessary for financial viability. For instance, I discovered that if you invest in a local business in the city of Philadelphia, you have the potential to earn a significant amount of interest on your money. This is because in the city of Philadelphia it is incredibly difficult to secure a license to serve liquor. This is frequently an issue of not having the fund to hire the necessary individuals to secure this license. If individuals would assist fund a restaurant to receive a liquor license, they would earn some share of all of the proceeds from the profits made off the sale of alcoholic beverages.

In the city that I live in, the requirements to obtain a liquor licence are not as stringent as those in other cities, and as a result, nearly all restaurants are able to serve alcoholic beverages if they so choose. I figured that there was no place for this investment opportunity in my own city, but I also knew that there was no harm in asking around. What I found was that several restaurants and retail establishments were seeking investors, and are really interested because this is a sort of capital investment that goes outside of banks. Loans for businesses that I found tended to be on a scale between one thousand and ten thousand dollars, making some of these investments quite large. I decided to get invested in two businesses: one was a local sporting goods store and the other was a restaurant. I invested one thousand dollars in the sporting goods store and two thousand in the restaurant.

With my money, both of these enterprises were able to expand. It is worth noting that the owners of these stores were also quite invested, but they used my investment to supplement the costs for making improvements to these stores. For the sporting goods store, they simply used the money to front the payment of new sporting goods for fencing. I thought this was odd until I found out the local high school had recently started a fencing team – the problem was that there was no where to buy the equipment. I'm not sure on the total cost of the equipment that was purchased through my local business, but I know that it was more than the one thousand dollars I lent them. Over the course of the following three months, I earned $220 on this investment, plus the base investment that I received back. Twenty-two percent interest on a one thousand dollar investment for three months without any monitoring is not bad at all, but the limitations to making this investment were that I had to reach out the business. I never would have found this opportunity if I didn't ask around my city and find out that this business was in need of investors. I believe this is the reason that I found myself in this position, as this investment seemed like such a good idea that I can't believe others hadn't taken the owner up on the investment. The truth is that the owner never asked any individuals for investments because they never thought that anyone would be willing to help them; they figured they would have to go to a bank. In this situation, everyone wins, and if I ever have kids I know that we'll get a great price on sporting equipment at a store that I was happy to invest in.

It turned out that the second investment in the restaurant was an even better deal than the first. This was an investment, and I, like everyone else, was perplexed as to why the proprietor of the restaurant hadn't been able to collect money from the other patrons. The proprietor of the restaurant, much like the owner of the sporting goods store, believed that soliciting investment from the customers of his establishment was inappropriate. I was surprised to see the owner's reaction when I asked him if he would accept my investment money on the condition that he detail for me precisely how he planned to put the funds to use. He told me that the restaurant would be using the money to build a deck in the back so that they could have more tables, expanding the amount of money that they could make in an hour, and also making the restaurant more desirable by having outside seating available. I was convinced, and over the course of the subsequent six months, I earned back my initial investment plus an additional $450 in interest, which works out to an annualized rate of return of 22.5% on a six-month investment. To reiterate, returns of this magnitude are exceedingly uncommon in the majority of markets. When I eat at that restaurant, the owner almost always comps me a drink or deducts the price of a side dish from my bill, so I end up paying significantly less than I ought to. In addition to this, I find that my check is almost always significantly lower than it should be. I'm not sure what the total cash value of this investment is, but the important thing is that it returned 22.5% in just six months and offered a number of other benefits in addition to those returns.

It's possible that using paper pockets to store Bit Coin is the most secure way to store crypto currency, but it's not 100% foolproof.

Utilizing various resources available online makes the creation of a paper wallet a real possibility. After that, it will generate a collection of public and private keys for you, both of which you will be able to print out on some paper for future reference.

You are the only person who will be able to access crypto currencies that have been stored at these addresses, and you must always have the piece of paper that contains the private key in your possession in order to do so.

Many people laminate these kinds of paper wallets and keep them hidden away in the safety deposit box at their financial institution or even at home in the safe. This helps them avoid having their personal information stolen. Since you will not be able to sell or trade Bit

Coin that is stored in these wallets, they are designed for the highest possible level of security as well as long-term investments.

The hardware wallet is a type of cold storage wallet that is increasingly common in people's everyday lives. An example of a hardware pocket is a USB power device, which can be used to store a person's non-public keys in a way that is both safe and secure. This is an example of a hardware pocket.

Cold wallets offer significant advantages over hot wallets in terms of security. These advantages stem from the fact that cold wallets are immune to any viruses that may be present on the computer of the user.

When utilizing a hardware wallet solution, personal keys are never made accessible for interaction with your network-connected machine or potentially vulnerable applications. This keeps your private information safe.

They are also frequently open source, which enables the network to determine their protection via code audits rather than relying on a third-party organization to certify that the device is safe to use. This eliminates the need for the network to pay for the certification.

When it comes to storing your Bitcoin or any other cryptocurrency, cold wallets are by far the most secure option.

Nevertheless, in order to operate at their fullest potential, they require a more comprehensive understanding of the installation procedure.

A correct way to install your wallets is to have all three of the following things: •An alternative account to shop with and sell from.

•A hot wallet, in which you can store low to medium amounts of cryptocurrency and use it to make purchases or sales.

• Cold storage pockets for keeping large amounts of items for extended periods of time.

Watch What You Say.

The words that we choose to use are a significant component of an inspirational perspective. Words are incredible and have the ability to perfectly describe our actions, as was established earlier on in this subsection. If we want to cultivate a prosperous mentality and, as a result, a prosperous life, we must first ensure that we are supporting that mindset by making effective use of language. Additionally, this will start with the beliefs that you hold.

Your subconscious compels your conscious mind to shape your statements in such a way that they conform to a pattern that is consistent with your core beliefs. For instance, if you have the preconceived notion that you are not competent or admirable enough to achieve a lofty goal, you might respond to a test by declaring, "I would never do that," and your actions will demonstrate that you are true to your belief that you are not capable of achieving the goal. However, it also works in the opposite direction, and the only way to find out if you don't try it is to. Therefore, you should position yourself for success by using your words appropriately.

In the diagram that follows, there are some examples of rich specialist words as well as examples of helpless specialist words. The following s will cover a significant portion of these concepts in greater detail.

Try looking into this matter. Pay close attention to the language you employ when speaking to specific individuals. Do they consist of rich specialist words or do they consist of helpless specialist words? CREATE YOUR OWN DISCIPLINE AND POSITIVE HABITS

The achievement of most goals, including freedom from the rat race, requires a significant amount of self-discipline on the part of the individual. In most cases, genuine self-discipline is required for a person to achieve the level of success that is required to complete professional tutoring or receive a postgraduate education. Assuming that mindset can be carried forward into the pursuit of wealth, it will serve you well in doing so.

The origin of discipline can be traced back to one's tendencies. Every one of us has developed a tendency. There are some that are excellent, and there are some that are not. It's a funny thing, but it seems like it's much simpler to develop poor schedules than it is to develop good ones. It's possible that I'll never fully understand that aspect of human instinct, other than the fact that we get pleasure from observing animals and that certain tendencies provide a shortcut to that end.

The formation of a habit takes 66 days on average, but this number can be shorter or longer for different individuals.7 REGARDLESS OF HOW LONG IT TAKES, you are able to convert another movement into an interaction that your cerebrum will recognize as being both typical and significant. That is a small price to pay for something that will benefit you for the rest of your life and bring you advancement opportunities.

Positive behaviors are consistent among wealthy people. In order to advance, it is necessary to engage in practices that are beneficial and to maintain the discipline necessary to carry on. Generally speaking, the happiest and richest people I've met are those who have a small number of deeply ingrained, abundance-creating designs that they follow every day. The majority are trivial and seem to be of no consequence, but their cumulative positive effects are long-lasting and substantial. The most well-known ones include making a commitment to one's own self-improvement, engaging in profound learning, being trustworthy, practicing meditation and concentration, rising early, and delegating responsibilities.

Developing a habit that is beneficial takes a lot of self-control, but once it's in place, that fresh approach to doing things will help you keep moving forward even when life throws roadblocks in your path. To break away from the education that got you ready for your career but didn't help you get rich requires a significant amount of self-control on the part of professionals.

The Three Genuine Forms Of Currency

Cash is the medium of exchange when purchasing necessities. Because I am in need of an apple, I am willing to exchange money for one. Because I am in desperate need of a home, I am willing to trade money for one. In the event that somebody needs something that I have, they can give me money in exchange for it.

Money, as its very name suggests, denotes something that is "ready for use." In the situations that were discussed earlier, cash is available to be used as a medium of exchange. Assuming that "available for use" is all that "cash" refers to, the question is whether or not cash is the only thing that can be considered a currency.

When most people think of money, their thoughts most likely turn to financial matters. However, when I consider everything that I do in my life, I can see very plainly that money is not the only form of currency that I use on a daily basis. In point of fact, I don't even rely primarily on that money. On any given day, it's likely that I'll be giving or receiving any one of the following three monetary standards, or some combination of them:

1. currency

 2. time

3. one's sanity

In the same way that I hand over cash in exchange for something, I can easily hand over some of my time in exchange for something. In exchange for something, I may be coerced into giving up some of the mental steadiness I have worked so hard to maintain.

Let's say I have a family room that needs some custom racks built for it. When it comes to having these racks constructed, I have two options:

1. Obtain the services of someone to build them for me.

2. I will construct them myself.

When it comes to a scenario like this one, the majority of people only focus on one thing, and that is money. The amount of money that could be saved by not employing someone to do anything is typically presented as the standard argument that opposes employing someone to do the activity. In light of this argument, I have arrived at the conclusion that I ought to set aside the money that I would pay another person to fabricate the racks, and instead do it myself.

I have two or three different thoughts running through my head regarding the construction of racks. To begin, I am completely clueless regarding the process of building racks. In addition, I don't have a natural talent for doing work of that nature. Because I'm not an exceptionally bright person, figuring out a way to construct them probably wouldn't come easily or normally to me. I've mentioned this before, but it bears repeating: I'm not particularly smart. The following thought that came to mind was that I do not particularly prefer to worry about things that I am terrible at and detest doing. A third idea is that because books are heavy, if I don't assemble the racks perfectly, I run the risk of the whole rack collapsing and detaching a piece of the divider when I fill it with books. This is assuming that I don't assemble the racks perfectly.

It is therefore unmistakable that in the event that I construct the racks on my own, I will pay for them with two things: my time and my mental lucidity. The time component would be a reality for anyone who built something by themselves, and the mental soundness component would be obvious to me as well as to anyone else who has absolutely no interest or innate ability in that kind of work. Along these lines, despite the fact that I have just put aside the money that I would have paid another person to assemble the racks, I have just purchased the racks using the two forms of currency that are less well-known: my time and my sanity.

Strategies That Are Most Effective For Day Trading

Let's take a look at some of the day trading strategies that have been the most successful. When applied correctly, these strategies can assist you in making a significant amount of additional income. It is possible to have a home run in certain circumstances. Please keep in mind that not all of these strategies are appropriate for high-frequency trading. As a result, you might find that you need to keep holding onto stocks for a few hours rather than a few minutes. Nevertheless, the profits have the potential to compensate for the loss.

Launch of operation

A stock breaking past a predetermined upper limit is what is meant by this strategy. A stock's ceiling is referred to as its "resistance level." Investors are reluctant to cross this psychological threshold because of the potential risks involved. In other words, market participants believe that this factor makes the stock price unreasonably high. On the other hand, there are times when investors are waiting for a certain event before making the decision to purchase the stock in question. For instance, investors might be waiting for data on the economy to be released by the government. If the data looks promising, they will enter the market. If the data is poor, they will maintain their position.

The point of entry: Examine the price history of the stock to establish where you want to get in at the beginning of this trade. If you discover that it had been sold at a higher price point in the past, you will have a point of reference for where the price may eventually settle. If you observe that the stock's price has approached the level of resistance but has not yet managed to go above it, the stock is getting ready to make a breakout. It is possible that the stock is now prepared to break through a level of resistance after it has done so three times in a row. Even though the timing is impossible to predict, all signs point to the fact that it will take place very quickly. Therefore, you should keep this in mind.

Exit point: You can get out of the trade at any point above the resistance level. This is your exit point. Setting your selling price at a level that is reasonable is a good general rule to follow. For instance, anything that is either very close to or exactly at its previous high is an excellent idea. It is in your best interest to maintain your position at the price's previous high unless there is a reason to believe that the price will break past its previous highs. It all depends on where you choose to enter the market. You might make a killing.

Change of direction

A trend reversal occurs when a stock's price is falling, then stops falling, and then starts rising again. On the other hand, the opposite is also true. As a result, reversals are extremely helpful both as entry and exit points in the market. You need to be familiar with the history of the stock's price in order to put this strategy into action. You can determine whether or not there will be a trend reversal based on this, as well as when it will happen.

Let's look at a pattern of deterioration. A "bearish" trend is another name for this trend. When a bearish trend is present, the price of a stock will eventually drop to a certain point before rebounding from that low point. It is not always easy to pinpoint the precise moment when something like this will take place. However, with the help of technical analysis, it is possible to pinpoint the exact moment at which a trend is about to change.

You need to look at the point at which the trendline stops falling and then starts to flatten out in order to identify the reversal point. After that, you will be able to identify the point at which the trendline will start to climb. The trendline may occasionally take the form of a "V" in certain situations. This indicates that it drops, strikes a point, and then immediately bounces back up to its original position. The point just before the price begins to rebound is the point at which you should make your entry. Because of this, the price at which you can purchase the stock is at its absolute lowest point before it starts to rise.

The opposite of a bearish trend is referred to as a "bullish" trend. When we see a trend like this, it indicates that the price is going up until it reaches a point where it will start going down again. Your best opportunity to make a sale is right at the point just before the price begins to fall again. As a result, this is the stage at which you will see the greatest increase in revenue.

When you use reversals, you have the ability to buy at the point that is the lowest possible price and then sell at the point that is the highest possible price. You can achieve the greatest possible profit by doing so.

The term "commodities"

The term "commodities" refers to unrefined components or vital rural goods, and commodity reserves invest resources in these categories.

Product prices are impacted in various ways by supply, demand, and even international affairs.

The following are some of the benefits that investors receive from having ware reserves:

• Diversification of investment holdings

• Provision of defence against growth. The prices of goods will almost always go up in line with expansion, which places it among a select few unique resources that stand to benefit from price increases brought on by inflation.

• The possibility of monetary advancement. The costs of the products go up and become more in line with market interests. When a product is in higher demand, its price will go up, which means that the investor will receive a greater return on their investment.

There is a diverse selection of item reserves available, including the following:

• Reserves for the index. These subsidies keep tabs on a list that contains a variety of various ware assets.

• Reserves of several commodities. These assets are directly deposited into the ware asset.

• Investment vehicles that are dependent on futures markets. Invest in potential customers' contract obligations while avoiding the purchase of actual physical assets.

Generally speaking, the goods that are traded can be categorised into the following four groups:

• Alluvial gold. Copper, gold, silver, and platinum are the precious metals. Gold has traditionally been considered a risk-free venture. The price of gold also tends to rise whenever there is widespread interest in a new expansion. It has served as an efficient means of preserving abundance throughout a considerable number of eras. You have the option of holding either coins or bars. There no appropriate response to this. Gold is considered to be an important component of any investment portfolio due to the fact that it reduces the level of risk that the rest of your speculations will be exposed to.

• Vitality. Include unrefined petroleum, oil that is used for warmth, combustible fuel and petrol.

• Meat and other forms of livestock

•Agricultural pursuits. Include ingredients such as corn, soybeans, wheat, rice, cocoa, espresso, cotton and sugar in your recipe.

The use of a prospective contract is one approach that may be utilised to invest resources into things. A valid agreement between two parties to transfer a particular ware resource at a set cost at a predetermined time in the future is known as a prospective contract.

The person who buys a destinies contract takes on the responsibility of ensuring that they will buy and obtain the essential item after the fates contract has run its course. At the time when the agreement is set to expire, the merchant is taking on the responsibility of delivering the fundamental good to the customer.

The following are some of the many benefits of investing resources in commodities:

• The promotion of diversity

• the possibility of profits • the possibility of protection from rising prices

Investing resources in commodities can have a number of drawbacks, including the following: • Prices can be unpredictable. • It can be influenced by events that occur in other parts of the world.

Claim procedures for commodities can be broken down into three categories:

• Buy futures contracts • Buy through a pooled asset or an exchange-traded fund (ETF) • Own the real goods itself

www.ingramcontent.com/pod-product-compliance
Lightning Source LLC
Chambersburg PA
CBHW071235210326
41597CB00016B/2058